SEOI-NAGE

Hidetoshi Nakanishi attacks with his specialty: *ippon-seoi-nage*.

Yoshiharu Minami attacks with his specialty: *morote-seoi-nage*.

JUDO MASTERCLASS TECHNIQUES

SEOI-NAGE
MOROTE-SEOI-NAGE   IPPON-SEOI-NAGE

HIDETOSHI NAKANISHI

Photographs by David Finch

Ippon Books

First Published in 1993
Second Edition (Revised): 1996

British Library Cataloguing in Publication Data

Nakanishi, Hidetoshi
Seoi-Nage: Judo Masterclass Techniques
1. Judo
2. Title

ISBN 0-9518455-4-3

ACKNOWLEDGEMENTS
Special thanks go to The Great Britain Sasakawa Foundation for its generous assistance towards this project.

My thanks go to the Kodokan, Tokyo for the loan of the dojo for the photo session.

I received additional information from many sources; but I would especially like to single out Nobuyuki Sato, my sensei at Tokai University, and Katsuhiko Kashiwazaki, head instructor at the International Budo University.

Extra demonstrations by Paul Ajala and Kogo Kimura

Additional Photography courtesy of Edward Ferrie and *Kindai Judo*.

Managing Editor: Nicolas Soames
Production Editor: Oon Oon Yeoh
Design & layout: Miles Holt
Photographer: David Finch
Printer: Redwood Books, Trowbridge, Wiltshire.

Ippon Books Ltd. (UK)
HR House,
447 High Road,
North Finchley,
London N12 OAF,
England.

Contents

Toshihiko Koga and his amazing *ippon-seoi-nage*.

Foreword

Seoi-nage is the single most popular throw in judo. Though primarily the technique, *par excellence*, for the smaller person, it is also used with considerable success by heavyweights. Part of its popularity lies in its efficiency—the principle of carrying a weight on the back is universal. But its success as a fighting technique is also due to its remarkable versatility.

Although there are some similarities between *morote-seoi-nage* and *ippon-seoi-nage*, there are many aspects which are unique to each. This can be seen by the way that most of those who become specialists in one form of *seoi-nage* seldom use the other.

However, there is sufficient common ground to include both techniques in one volume. The author, Hidetoshi Nakanishi, demonstrates *ippon-seoi-nage* himself. For the *morote-seoi-nage* he specially invited his compatriot, Yoshiharu Minami, a double world champion, to do the demonstrations.

The result has, I think, proved immensely interesting. For a start, the judo styles of these two world champions are markedly different even though they both grew up in the central Japanese judo tradition. As can be seen, Minami possesses an unsullied classical style: his *morote-seoi-nage* is based on flexibility, movement, control and timing.

Nakanishi's judo is firmly rooted in Japanese tradition and has these qualities too; but, as his demonstrations show, he has made a virtue of the modern style only too readily dismissed as 'power judo'. The fascinating contrasts between these two men demonstrates the richness of judo itself.

Minami and Nakanishi came together one day in the Kodokan to demonstrate the techniques for this book. First of all, they went through the basics and fundamentals of their techniques. Next came the combination and counters. Then, came a more relaxed session, when both went through their repertoire of more unusual variations. Nakanishi, in particular, seemed to have an inexhaustable fund of ideas collected during his decades of intensive judo both in Japan and abroad.

For those of us who were there, it was an unforgettable experience. We hope this book captures the searching spirit of that day, and will prove a useful vehicle for enriching a technical understanding of the *seoi-nage* specialist.

Nicolas Soames
Masterclass Series Editor

An old Japanese *ju-jutsu* illustration featuring a standing form of *ippon-seoi-nage*.

History of Seoi-Nage

Seoi-nage is regarded throughout the judo world as **the** classical judo throw. More than any other throw in the judo canon, it represents the ideal technique with which a small man can throw a big man—the principle which is at the very heart of judo philosophy and practice.

The word *seoi* suggests the image of "carrying on the back". To the Japanese mind it suggests carrying a heavy load in an efficient and relatively effortless manner: the strain is taken by a combination of good posture, strong thighs, and a light balance. These qualities are promoted by the characteristic Japanese body-type: short arms and short legs. The legs, always seen as playing a major role in *seoi-nage*, are developed by a lifetime of getting up from sitting on the floor—very different from a life spent getting out of chairs. This cultural factor still determines the difference between the Japanese *seoi-nage* and the way it is practised in the West.

"Back-carry" was a feature of Japanese life for centuries. This was partly because of the mountainous nature of the country and partly because it was only in the 19th century that roads were sufficiently well developed to take greater volumes of wheeled traffic. Instead, Japanese roads, such as the famous Tokaido from Tokyo to Nagoya were filled with riders and pedestrians carrying loads upon their backs. Aristocrats and the rich rode or were carried in palanquins rather than travelling in wagons or coaches.

This variaton is referred to as *seoi-otoshi*, probably because of the wide stance of the *tori*.

The *ju-jitsu* schools drew on this experience of carrying to create two different throwing techniques. One was *morote-seoi-nage*. It was known, in many different schools, by a variety of names including *seoi-goshi*, although the term *seoi-nage* would have been generally understood. Even in the early days of judo it was sometimes called *nihon-seoi-nage* or *eri-seoi-nage*. The name of *morote-seoi-nage* was a comparatively recent development. However it did not feature in the first *Gokyo*, a catalogue of 40 principal throws, drawn up in 1895. *Seoi-nage* did feature in

Dai Ikkyo, the first set in the *te-waza* section, but it was taught in the form of *ippon-seoi-nage*.

Morote-seoi-nage was of more limited use. Not really a technique that was of practical use on the Japanese battlefield against an armoured opponent, it evidently emerged to make the most of the Japanese kimono. Yet many of the *ju-jitsu* schools practised with short sleeve *judogi*, making *morote-seoi-nage* difficult to bring off. The introduction of long-sleeved *judogi* of relatively loose design made a great difference; it was then that *morote-seoi-nage* came into its own.

An additional factor that helped to bring *morote-seoi-nage* into its own was the lack of weight categories in the early days. It is the technique par excellence for a small man to use on a big man. This is one reason why *morote-seoi-nage* is invariably the first technique taught to Japanese children, or at the start of most judo careers. It is regarded as a good throw through which one can learn the basics of breaking the balance, turning in and throwing.

Yoshiharu Minami, who demonstrates *morote-seoi-nage* in this book, has the classic build for this throw. Standing at only 160 cm, he grew up in the early days of weight category judo. But most of his practice was done in the *dojo* where everyone was expected to train together regardless of size or weight. In discussion, Minami emphasizes repeatedly the importance of doing *randori* with bigger men in the understanding of *morote-seoi-nage* . He feels that if he had not had this background he woudl not have had the success with the throw that he did.

Ippon-seoi-nage is a somewhat different matter. Tradition links it less with the action of carrying loads on the back than with the carrying of the palanquin. There is certainly a similarity of posture, with one arm upright to take the pole. Of course, the

Two early versions of *ippon-seoi-nage*.

formal *ippon-seoi-nage* carries the load not on the shoulder, where the pole of the palanquin would be borne, but on the back, with the raised arm around the opponent's biceps. However, the principle of lifting with the raise arm can be seen to be common to both actions. The word used within the palanquin context is *katsugu*, which denotes lifting up using the shoulder. The mere fact that *ippon-seoi-nage* is not dependent upon a *kimono* or jacket makes it more versatile (though there is no doubt that clothes make it easier to do).

Various versions of the *ippon-seoi-nage* exists in many wrestling traditions. In modern free-style wrestling in the West it is called "the flying mare"; it is also used in Greco-Roman wrestling as well as in Sambo wrestling, the Russian style established between the two world wars. It even exists in *sumo* wrestling where it is referred to as *seoi-nage* or simply *oi-nage*. Judo has borrowed from *sumo* the idea of *soto-muso* where the hand is used to sweep or block the opponent's thigh.

These are the two main forms of *seoi-nage* and they have existed side by side in judo throughout its growth into a world-wide sport.

One of their many points of similarity is a continuing and considerably controversy that evolves around the use of "the drop-down" variation. *Seoi-nage* had its tradition of dropping in Japan from the early days. Generally, it amounted to falling down on one knee and springing up again to throw. In *Judo Nippon Tamashi*, a volume published in 1905, which collected various *ju-jitsu* techniques, *seoi-nage* is described as a long throw, projecting the opponent, and *seoi-otoshi* as a short throw, pulling the opponent over. Perhaps even now, the distinction has relevance.

But dropping onto both knees—which has existed in judo as long as anyone can remember—has always been regarded as a

Ippon-seoi-nage exists in sumo as well.

日本相撲──負投(おいなげ)綾川五郎次「一味清風」

An early photo of the sumo application of *ippon-seoi-nage*. Notice that the *tori* is a small player.

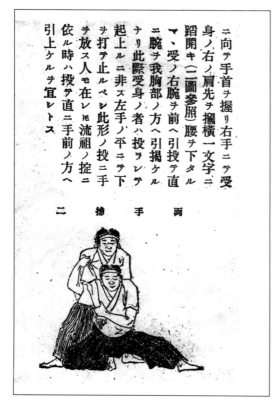

二向テ手首ヲ握リ右手ニテ受
身ノ右ノ肩先ヲ搗横一文字ニ
蹈開キ（一圖参照）腰ヲ下タル
マ、受ノ右腕ヲ前ヘ引投テ直
ニ腕ヲ我胸部ノ方ヘ引揚ケル
ナリ此際受身ノ者ハ投ヲレテ
起上ルニ非ズ左手ノ平ニテ下
ヲ打テ止ルベシ此形ノ投ニ手
ヲ放ス人モ在レド流祖ノ掟ニ
依ル時ハ投ヲ直ニ二手前ノ方ヘ
引上ケルヲ宜シトス

二　捕　手　両

Here we see a drop-knee variation
of the *ippon-seoi-nage*.

rule, Japan hopes to maintain an overall
high standard of basic judo technique,
rather than give a handful of individuals
the satisfaction of bringing home a few
medals.

However, it must be said that as much as
80 per cent of *seoi-nage* seen in international
competition are of the drop-down
variation. There are, of course, considerable
variety within the umbrella term of *drop-seoi-nage*.

Nevertheless, *seoi-nage*, in all its forms
continues to be not only one of the most
successful techniques in competition and
randori, but also one of the most dynamic
and satisfying—to do and watch. This
alone will ensure its continued position as
one of the most popular techniques in the world.

Here is a drop-knee version of *morote-seoi-nage*.

lesser form, or even a bad form. Any young
person who does it in a Japanese dojo will
be severely criticized even now, for it is
regarded as potentially damaging to their
knees. Numerous competitors have
damaged knees as a result of the wear and
tear of judo practice. Frequently dropping
on the knees certainly doesn't help to keep
them in good shape.

Currently in Japan, competitors under the
age of 16 (junior high school and under) are
forbidden to attempt a drop-down *seoi-nage*
on both knees, in competition. With this

MOROTE–SEOI-NAGE

Yoshiharu Minami

Morote-Seoi-Nage: A Personal View

Yoshiharu Minami was born in Hiroshima in Western Honshu, the central island of Japan. His grandfather taught judo in Shinoguchi Dojo, one of the *machi-dojo* (town dojos) in Hiroshima, and he began his practice at the age of 10.

He started with *morote-seoi-nage*, and it has remained with him ever since as his *tokui-waza*, his favourite technique. He was small as a boy—in maturity he stands at just 160 cm. He was also very light, so it was only natural that he should follow in the tradition of *morote-seoi-nage* specialists. The throw both attracted him and suited him. He developed a freely moving style, producing the throw from many different angles, but always in a pattern of movement rather than a static attack. He often used *de-ashi-barai* as an additional technique with helped to get even the biggest opponents moving.

Though Minami has always been light, generally among the smallest and lightest in every competition he has fought in—he learned to use his body weight well. This is a feature that can be seen throughout his demonstration photographs: the way he hangs on to *uke* to bring him forward, or moves him backwards with a dynamic whole-body explosion, shows Japanese judo at its most exemplary.

When he was 15 years old he won his first major tournament—the Junior High School Tournament of Hiroshima Prefecture. The event was divided into three weight categories, and though he fought in the lightweight category, he was by far the smallest and the lightest. He used *morote-seoi-nage* in all his fights, concluding with an *ippon* score in the final. It was a pattern that was to be repeated many times in his forthcoming competitive career.

When he was 18, he won the Inter-High School National Championships. He had seven contests and won four of them, including the final with *morote-seoi-nage* for *ippon*. He left school and went to work for a steel company with a successful judo club, and he is still employed there. By this time his judo was largely fully-formed.

By 1973, he had proved himself, with the help of his *morote-seoi-nage*, the leading lightweight in Japan, and he was selected to represent his country in the world championships in Lausanne. By this time he had added left *ippon-seoi-nage* and *kouchi-gari* to his repertoire.

The early rounds of the category proved relatively easy with *morote-seoi-nage* always to the fore. In the semi-final he met his first really strong international opponent, the Russian Pitschelauri. Minami admits now that before the contest he was a little concerned because the Russian had looked very capable. When they met, however, Minami threw his opponent in 14 seconds with *morote-seoi-nage*. It was, he says now, one of the best techniques he ever did because the timing was exact. He went on to win the event, beating Kawaguchi in the final.

In 1975 he won the All-Japan Weight Category Championships and was again selected to represent Japan in the World Championships, this time in Vienna. He won every fight to the final with *ippon* and once again *morote-seoi-nage* featured prominently. He either scored *ippon* with it, or it got him a part-score, leaving him to conclude the matter on the ground. In the final he met his compatriot Katsuhiko Kashiwazaki. They both knew each other's techniques well, and the beginning proved quite static. But it concluded with the inevitable *morote-seoi-nage* for *waza-ari*, with a second consecutive world title for Minami.

Minami still works for the Shinitetsu Steel Company, but is also a coach on Japan's National Men's Squad, working with the lightweights. He says now that, apart from large numbers of *uchikomi*, and attention to correct detail, his *morote-seoi-nage* was developed by fighting bigger men. "*Morote-seoi-nage* is a very difficult technique," he admits. "Many smaller people find it easier to do *tai-otoshi* or *uchimata*. But if you are serious about developing *morote-seoi-nage*, then you must practise with bigger men. This is really the way to learn it."

a) Minami drops down low on one knee.

b) Minami pulls strongly with his *hikite*.

c) Mariani is pulled over and lands largely on his back. *Waza-ari scored.*

Minami was one of a group of outstanding Japanese exponents of *morote-seoi-nage* in the 1970's. The others included Toyokazu Nomura and Shozo Fujii. All three were noted for their abilities to spring up after dropping down rather than merely dropping down and pulling or rolling their opponents over. On this controversial point Minami comments: "Even whe I was young, many players in Japan merely dropped down onto their knees. Sometimes I did so too, but only very lightly and with my toes tucked under, so that, in a split second, I was able to spring up again, with my opponent well loaded onto my back. Using *morote-seoi-nage* in a contest situation is not easy, especially when your opponent is bent over in a very low defensive posture. But I still believe that it is best not to drop hard onto your knees. At least I can say that at the age of 40, I have two world titles and I still have both cartilages in my knees."

d) Minami strikes again, this time his left knee actually comes off the ground.

e) The strong pull...

f) ...*waza-ari-awasatte-ippon!*

Morote-Seoi-Nage: The Basics

The Fundamentals

Though *morote-seoi-nage* and *ippon-seoi-nage* are quite distinctive in terms of grips, they share many characteristics by virtue of their "back-carry" origin. These links include the basic posture, *kuzushi* and stepping patterns, as well as combinations and even counters. Familiarity with this common ground is important to provide a basis for an understanding of the whole *seoi-nage* concept.

Shisei (Posture)
This is the basic position for both *morote-*

seoi-nage and *ippon-seoi-nage*. I am standing in front of *uke*, my feet shoulder-width apart. I am balanced lightly but equally on both feet, with more weight on my toes than my heels.

I should be able to rock gently forward and back. Ideally, my feet are in line with *uke*'s shoulders, while his feet are slightly wider apart. My back is straight—not straight up to the ceiling, but at an angle to the ground. Most importantly, there is no curvature to the spine. A final guide-line is that, seen from the side, my belt must be lower than *uke*'s. This way, my hips can become a fulcrum, the centre of gravity.

Kuzushi (Breaking of Balance)
It is important to understand the correct breaking of balance right at the beginning

of a *seoi-nage* study. More *seoi-nage* attempts fail through insufficient or incorrect *kuzushi* than anything else. I do not want to come in with my back so tightly against *uke* that there is no room to bring him forward. When *seoi-nage* is taught, good body contact is always emphasized, but sometimes at the expense of space, which is just as crucial. There must be a small gap between *uke* and myself so that I can draw him forward unimpeded onto his toes. (It also allows me space to make the turn in the first place). I must also get the direction of the *kuzushi* right. In *seoi-nage*, I am always pulling *uke* over his toes. Under the pressure of competition or *randori* this may vary somewhat but this basic rule should apply. If you draw a line across your partner's toes, you throw at right-angles to that line. It is as simple as that. Here *uke*'s feet are parallel to the line of the mat. I can throw him straight ahead. If his left foot was slightly back, my position and my *kuzushi* would have to take account of this and I would have to alter the line of throw lightly to the left. In short, it is my aim to harmonize my body position and throwing direction with my opponent.

Uke is drawn onto this straight back and, by pulling on the hands, is fixed to my back. Once there I shoud be able to walk round quite comfortably with my partner on my back, bearing the weight on my hips and legs.

At the very least, I should be able to rock forward brining *uke* off his feet. Note that despite the temptations, I have not bent my back to do this. In my opinion, this correct action comes more easily to Japanese people, who are accustomed to

rising from a sitting position on the floor
than to Western people who are more
reliant upon chairs, and therefore use their
thigh muscles less.

I try not to bend my back even when I off-
load *uke*. The feeling is more of a twist but
is is actually quite a complex affair. There
are many varying factors, including *uke's*
height relative to mine.

The traditional teaching isolates three
points:

i) I raise his body—in the demonstration
position, by pulling his hands upwards
and even outwards.

ii) The general direction of the pull is
forwards.

iii) Only then do I turn and put a twist on
the action. As I direct my partner onto his
back you can see my back is still not bent.

Kumite

The Japanese break grips down into various classifications. They do this at the level of basic techniques and find it particularly useful for instant analysis of a situation or a problem.

a) **Hikite** is the sleeve grip. The pull must be high and smooth. It has been called "the long pull".

b) **Tsurite** is the lapel or collar grip. The initial action is generally more of a lifting motion. The word *tsuri* comes from the root "to fish" and suggests the image of a bent fishing rod pulling a fish from the water.

c) **Ai-Yotsu** refers to same side grips—left against left or right against right. It is essential to be aware of your opponent's grip. Almost every technique will vary slightly according to whether you are facing an opponent with the same side grip (e.g. you are both left-handers) or an opposing grip (left against right). Some techniques will work superbly in one case and not at all with the others.

d) **Kenka-Yotsu** refers to opposing grips—left against right. It is, to be colloquial, a whole different ball game.

Mawari (Turn)

There are two basic stepping patterns for the attack—*ushiro mawari* (reverse turn) and *mae-mawari* (front turn). There are, of course, many other stepping patterns, but they are generally variations of this theme. In *ushiro-mawari* you retreat, bringing *uke* onto you. In *mae-mawari*, you step forward into the attack, effectively slipping past the defences of his arms. These are discussed in detail at the beginning of each section on *morote-seoi-nage* and *ippon-seoi-nage*. Most specialists will tend to favour one or the otehr but will be at the very least competent in both. Under the pressure of competition, the distinction between the two may blur; nevertheless, it is advisable to gain a good understanding of both in a steady rhythmn, knowing their special characteristics, before advancing to the mixed stepping patterns.

Hikite (sleeve grip)

The sleeve pull: it has been described as the long pull. It must be smooth and high, with the little finger and outside edge of the hand twisting upwards to gain extra height. Tradition regards this as the most important pull. It takes considerable practice to achieve a good *hikite*—but then it is of service in many other techniques as well.

a) The main obstacle to the *hikite* pull is the high grip which effectively blocks the turn before it has even started. *Uke* takes a high collar grip and, as can be seen, Minami cannot turn his head. His answer is to free his left hand and take hold of *uke*'s forearm.

b) He pushes away with both hands. The movement is a sudden explosion, not just with the hands, but with the whole body alive and moving backwards.

c) The effect can be seen in the way Minami is now standing upright. He is free to attack. This is a basic gripping tactic that must be learned.

d) Minami takes back his *tsurite* grip and turns into the space. This is a kind of mixed turn...somewhere in between *ushiro* and *mae-mawari*.

e) *Uke* cannot resist being taken into the air and over.

Tsurite (lapel grip)

There is no doubt that the main problem all *morote-seoi-nage* specialists face is winning the freedom necessary to get the tsurite grip into throwing position. Folding it into place feels slightly awkward at first. But once the basic knack is mastered it offers tremendous control and reserves of power. However, it must be said that there is a danger of elbow injury with *morote-seoi-nage*. The way to avoid this is by observing correct procedure.

Note: the greater the break of balance with the sleeve grip and the short pull of the lapel grip, the more he can afford to fold his arm towards uke's armpit, aiming for an an ultimately very high lift. But, if tori aims for the armpit without such a strong kuzushi, he will be in danger of being sent backwards. It is best to aim for the inner elbow.

a) The first important point is the angle of the tsurite arm when it is gripping the lapel: the hand should always be higher than the elbow. This allows the arm to be bent in position without endangering the elbow joint. It offers safety against injury even if the opponent pulls back in defence.

b) The initial movement of the *tsurite* hand is to pull *uke* slightly forwards with the hand and wrist. This helps to initiate *kuzushi*, and also to give *tori* space to turn his wrist, winding it into the cloth. This is the best method, and offers some protection to the elbow. Sometimes it is not possible, and the hand is bent back. If the thumb is relaxed, the position is not too dangerous for the elbow. Then, bringing the elbow into the side, the turn can be made. The turn should never be made with an open armpit.

c) Minami stresses that the process of folding the *tsurite* arm into place should occur simultaneously with the stepping pattern. It is all about total body movement. As soon as the throwing position is achieved, the elbow can start to lift up.

d) In the harsher reality of *randori* or competition, this is not easy: uke takes a firm grip on the sleeve by the elbow and tries to stop the arm bending into place. What often happens is that *tori*'s arm gets left behind his own body, where it is weak.

e) This is the correct action. Minami has pulled with his left hand to bend *uke* forward a bit more and then lead with his elbow. He is aiming to put his left forearm more or less in the crook of *uke*'s elbow.

f) Another important aspect of this precision placing of the elbow is that *tori* needs room to complete the turn. Here, he has left himself sufficient room to do this.

g) The moment of *kuzushi*. Note the *hikite* grip complementing the *tsurite*.

Basic Versions

Ushiro-Mawari (reverse turn)

This is generally the first technique taught in Japan. It follows the basic judo principle of yielding before and oncoming force in order to take control. Minami uses thi particularly when facing much bigge opponents.

a) *Uke* is coming forward, and Minami i retreating—but with purpose. Though clearly smaller and lighter than his partner he is preparing to put his whole momentum into the coming technique.

b) Springing powerfully off his left leg, he pulls high with his hikite grip (sleeve hand). The right elbow is high and the little finger of the hand turned up to the ceiling Despite the disparity in size, this action brings *uke* onto his left foot. It also opens a space for Minami to turn into for the completion of his technique. The timing is smooth and harmonious—Minami's right foot and *uke*'s left foot have come forward together in the same line.

c) This is the ideal *kuzushi*. *Uke*'s balance is completely broken—he is off both heels equally and can only tip forwards. Hidden behing uke's arm is the action of Minami's tsurite grip (the lapel grip). He has pulled forward to keep *uke* coming onto him, then slightly across to bring his elbow in place. It is a characteristic of *morote-seoi-nage* that it needs this amount of space in which to get into position.

d) *Uke* is brought unusually high onto Minami's back. However, Minami's posture and balance is perfect and he carries the weight effortlessly.

e) It is easy to despatch *uke*.

Mae-Mawari (front turn)

This is a marginally more difficult entry for a number of reasons. First of all, tori has to keep uke coming forward while he is himself moving in the opposite direction; secondly, he has to ensure there is sufficient space to turn and get his tsurite arm into position. Minami used this method himself when fighting opponents in his own weight category.

a) Minami turns in, bringing in his left foot in front of *uke*. As he does so, his *hikite* (sleeve grip) lifts high—his weight is on his right foot as he does so. He needs to have enough space to make his turn, yet not be so far away that he will be pulled backwards by *uke*.

b) Now he completes his turn. Note how his feet are just in front of *uke*, more or less in line with *uke*'s shoulders.

c) He squats low. As his body weight drops, he continues to pull *uke* forward. A bigger *kuzushi* is generally needed with *mae-mawari*.

d) to take *uke* over his shoulders, Minami stands and rocks forward…

e) …and throws.

Inside Grip

From a *kenka-yotsu* situation, *uke* has got the top grip. It is important that *tori* is able to shake off that grip in order to be able to get past his defences. The way to do so is to generally unsettle *uke* by pushing, pulling, manoeuvering him around.

a) When the time is right, Minami makes his entry. As he does so he flicks his left elbow upwards to help create the space he needs to do *morote-seoi-nage*.

b) He enters into the technique.

c) That little flick actually helps him to get past *uke*'s defending arms.

d) With the space already created, Minami drops down low underneath *uke*.

e) He projects upwards and *uke* is thrown—actually more to the side than to the front.

Inside Grip II

As seen from a different angle.

a) Minami uses his hands firmly. He open*s uke*'s defences by pushing his left hand over *uke*'s right shoulder, palm upwards.

b) The opening has allowed Minami to drop under.

c) *Uke* is thrown over.

Outside Grip

here is no doubt that it is much more
ifficult to do *morote-seoi-nage* from an
outside grip. But there are times when you
are forced into this situation.

Minami has let go of his *hikite* grip in
rder to provide a better view of the
ripping situation. Although it is *uke* who
as got the inside grip, Minami has
ctually changed the situation by bringing
is whole left arm over *uke*'s right arm. It is
rucial that you bring your **entire** left arm
ver so that you now have the inside
side grip. If you only get part of your
m over, you cannot properly turn in for
e throw.

Minami raises *uke*'s arm to create the
ace necessary for the turn. This action
so creates the momentum necessary to
ving his left arm across and place it into
e *morote-seoi-nage* position.

He tucks his left elbow into place while
opping low. Notice that he is also pulling
rongly with his *hikite* hand.

Special Variations

Drop Knee Morote-Seoi-Nage

In Japan, this variation is sometimes called by its old name: *kata-hiza-tsuki-seoi*. It allows *tori* to get down very low underneath *uke*'s centre of gravity t produce a powerful break of balanc before springing up to make the throw.

a) Having made his entry on one knee, Minami is in a good position: deep underneath uke and in between his legs. Although it is not obvious, the toes of his left foot are curled under. This will allow him to spring upwards powerfully when the time comes for him to do so.

b) Here he does exactly that. *Uke*'s balanc was only slightly broken, but as Minam projects upwards, he pulls strongly wit both his sleeve and lapel grips. As he rise *uke* is tipped forward sharply.

c) Minami gains impressive height with his throw while retaining control.

Katsuki of Japan performs *morote-seoi-otoshi* against Landart of France.
1978 Tournoi de Paris.

Morote-Seoi-Otoshi

Seoi-otoshi is without doubt the most successful variation of *morote-seoi-nage* in modern competition. Even though most traditionalists criticize its use—both in terms of poor form and potential knee damage—most champions who use *morote-seoi-nage*, apply this form. In *seoi-* *otoshi*, the opponent is actually pulle over—there is no lift involved. It is ve effective because the sudden low dro involved allows *tori* to dispense with th complex formalities of creating *kuzus* The surprise factor, particularly with a ta *tori*, can be great.

a) A good *seoi-otoshi* attack must be precise and as accurate as a standi attack. The object is to quickly get de between *uke*'s legs.

b) Note Minami's perfect positioning, as drops low.

c) Minami's strong pull loads *uke* onto his back.

d) Minami continues pulling strongly...

e) ...and *uke* is pulled over without the need for Minami to rise.

Cross Grip Morote-Seoi-Nage

There are many reasons why *kata-eri-seoi-nage* is a very successful competition technique. The problems of the *tsurite* hand are lessened considerably and by taking the lapel on the same side as the sleeve grip, the turn is much easier. It particularly useful against talle opponents, enabling *tori* to tuck in an turn with great speed, developir considerable torque.

a) Minami begins with a cross grip and turns into the attack. Notice that there is a lot of room for him to do so because of the cross grip stance.

b) *Uke* is loaded onto Minami's back.

c) Minami has straightened his legs and begins despatching *uke* towards the front and left hand side.

d) *Uke* is thrown cleanly onto his back.

Shota Chochosvili of the Soviet Union throws his Japanese opponent, Fumio Sasahara with a cross-grip *morote-seoi-nage*. Notice that Chochosvili has actually lifted his left leg in the air to aid with the rotation.

Single Sleeve Morote-Seoi-Nage

There are many occassions when a morote-seoi-nage specialist is denied his *tsurite* hold. *Kata-sode-seoi-nage* allows him to turn

inside the elbow, which will feel mor familiar to him than *ippon-seoi-nage*.

a) With his left foot already forwar Minami pulls on the *hikite* hand slightly t create the space for his attack.

b) He pivots on his left foot and begins th turn.

c) His left and is placed on the crook uke's elbow as he begins lowering hims underneath *uke*.

d) *Uke* is tipped forward and loaded onto Minami's back.

e) From here it is difficult to stop himself from being thrown.

Double Sleeve Morote-Seoi-Nage

This variation is actually an application of *sode-tsuri-komi-goshi* but in feeling, it is very similar to *morote-seoi-nage*. The beauty of the technique is that it will work left or right, *ai-yotsu* or *kenka-yotsu*.

a) I begin by holding the ends of both sleeves.

b) *Uke* is trapped because his arms are crossed. Notice that I have dropped down low, bending my knees.

c) I load him onto my back...

d) ...and unload him by straightening my legs.

Single Lapel Morote-Seoi-Nage

This is the kind of technique that people hear about or read about with great scepticsim. And then comes along a fighter such as Toshihiko Koga to prove that it can be done, and against some of the best fighters in the world.

a) It is common in contest for both fighters to be in an extreme *kenka-yotsu* stance with both denying the other a sleeve grip. Minami uses this to full advantage by quickly turning into *uke* with only a tsurite grip.

b) *Uke* doesn't expect this so his reaction is slow. This gives Minami the opportunity he needs to make a deep entry, which is crucial for a one-handed technique like this.

c) Minami pulls *uke* strongly over his hips with his *tsurite* grip.

d) It is a sensational technique. By the time *uke* realizes what has happened he is already flying over.

e) *Uke* is flat on his back.

Double Lapel Morote-Seoi-Nage

If *tori* cannot get his *hikite* grip it is possible to execute *morote-seoi-nage* from a double lapel grip.

a) Minami begins the attack by leading with his right leg. This gives *uke* the impression that he is about to execute a right handed attack.

b) Suddenly he spins into position. This creates a centripetal force that acts like a spring to allow tori to get past defensive arms.

c) *Uke* is loaded onto Minami's back, which acts as a fulcrum over which *uke* will be rotated.

d) Minami straightens his legs and continues with the strong pull. *Uke* will be thrown flat on his back.

a) The inimitable Angelo Parisi of France throws Vladimir Kocman of Czechoslovakia with his unique version of *morote-seoi-nage*.

b) Notice the doube laple grip.

a) Parisi, who was ambi-dextrous, could easily switch from left to right. This time, we see him throwing Zinnekar of Switzerland to the left.

b) He doesn't quite load his opponent onto his back, rather, he blocks him with his extended right leg—technically a *morote-seoi-otoshi*.

c) The result is just as devastating.

Combinations into Morote-Seoi-Nage

Ouchi-Gari into Morote-Seoi-Nage

This is a classic push-reaction combination that works surprisingly well.

a) Minami starts his entry. This is the beginning of his *ouchi-gari* attack.

b) He goes in and lightly taps *uke*'s right inner leg. This is more of a feint than a real attack.

d) Minami begins his turn and starts dropping low at the same time. Notice that his is pulling upwards and outwards with his *hikite*.

e) Minami is now right below *uke*. His left arm is tucked snugly under *uke*'s left armpit and his right arm is strongly pulling downwards. Notice how *uke* is tipped way off balance.

c) *Uke* responds by retreating. This creates the space necessary for the attack.

f) Minami despatches him by standing up and rotating him forwards.

Kouchi-Gari into Morote-Seoi-Nage

Balance, purpose, skill and a clear ultimate goal are necessary for success in combination techniques.

a) Minami begins the attack up with a *kouchi-gari*.

c) *Uke* steps off to avoid the attack and thus leaves the space Minami needs for a *morote-seoi-nage* attack.

d) Minami drops down low…

e) …and throws *uke*.

Kosoto-Gari into Morote-Seoi-Nage

standard combination for a *kenka-yotsu* tuation. The key to this technique is in making subtle downward pressure with the hands hile attacking with *kosoto-gari*. Maintain the ownward pressure—almost as if you were hanging on to him—so that *uke* feels he is being bent over as he retreats. When he tries to straighten up, release the pressure and drop underneath him to do a *morote-seoi-nage* attack.

Minami attacks with a determined *kosoto-ri*. It is a real attack, not a feint, so *uke* must p back in order to avoid being thrown.

b) *Uke* pulls backwards but Minami hangs on to him.

Minami immediately drops under...

e) ...and throws him with *morote-seoi-nage*.

Sasae-Tsuri-Komi-Ashi into Morote-Seoi-Nage

This is a good method to inveigle one's opponent in a particular direction—in this case, directly into the path of *morote-seoi-nage*.

a) Minami attacks with *sasae-tsuri-komi-ashi* to *uke*'s right shin.

b) His timing is good, and *uke* nearly goes over

d) This brings *uke* right into the path of *morote-seoi-nage*. Minami begins his attack by pivoting on his left foot…

e) …and dropping down perfectly into position for *morote-seoi-nage*. Minami's sudden descending bodyweight and pulling action of his hands completely destroys *uke*'s balance.

Uke has to take a large step towards 1ami's left in order to avoid falling over.

1inami stands up and completes the throw.

Combinations from Morote-Seoi-Nage

Morote-Seoi-Nage into Kuchiki-Daoshi

This technique relies on a strong defensive reaction from *uke* and a change in both direction and level of attack. The sudde switch catches *uke* by surprise.

a) Minami spins in for a drop *morote-seoi-nage* attack.

b) Although he is deep in between *uke*'s leg *uke* is resisting strongly.

c) Minami immediately turns and grabs *uke*'s left leg. Added power comes from a strong push with his left hand.

d) *Uke* is thrown backwards.

Morote-Seoi-Nage into Kouchi-Gari

is advisable to make a few *morote-seoi-nage* feints before actually attacking with a
cisive *kouchi-gari*.

Minami pulls downwards as if creating
entry for a *mae-mawari* style *morote-seoi-*
3e.

b) It is just a feint. Minami puts his left arm into
position for a fraction of a second, but he has
not committed his lower body.

This enables him to switch into a full-
oded *kouchi-gari* as *uke* is pulling back
inst the expected *morote-seoi-nage*.

d) As *uke*'s leg is clipped away both hands
drive his back towards the mat. *Ippon* is
inevitable.

Defences and Counters

As with any other judo throw, controlling the opponent's grip is the earliest and safest form of defence. Of course preventing him from gripping is deemed negative in competition and is certainly not something that should be over emphasized in *randori*. It is more acceptable to allow the opponent to grip and then neutralize his technique when he actually attempts to attack.

It is potentially very dangerous to allow an expert to grip as he wishes and let him attack with his favourite techniques. However, particularly in *randori*, it is good practice to try and find defences based o movement and on counter attack particularly as the less than perfect attac allows for a variety of possible counter *Sukui-nage* and *tani-otoshi* are clea possibilities, but it is worth experimentin with stepping around the initial attack an countering. Hirobumi Matsud lightweight world champion in 1965 was very agile uchimata specialist wh developed his own spectacularly effecti counter to *seoi-nage* using *uchimata*. It is question of training, imagination, willingness to take risks, and confidence.

Block the tsurite

Block the *tsurite*: the easiest, safest and perhaps most effective method, which doesn't let the spin of a *seoi-nage* attack start to develop. Against the left-hander, *tori*'s right hand shoves the elbow down to *uke*'s side.

Break the hikite

a) Uke turns in.

b) To defend, twist at the hips, pull t shoulder back, and tear the *hikite* free.

Uranage Counter

Uke attacks with drop *seoi-nage*.

b) *Tori* starts to step around *uke*'s attack.

As *uke* rises to try to gain some lift, *tori* ntinues to step around.

d) He grips *uke* with his free right hand and uses *uke*'s own impetus to twist him over his outstretched leg.

Uke is thrown with a low *uranage*, or if he pulling down too powerfully, *yoko-ruma*.

Morote-Seoi-Nage: Training

Morote-seoi-nage is a difficult throw to master. It requires speed and precision of movement as with most judo throws, but in addition the exponent has to overcome the quite considerable problems presented by the *tsurite* grip. Minami explains that he devoted thousands of hours in his early years to *uchikomi*, and he says unequivocally that the work has to be done: the movement pattern has to be drilled into the body so that it can be reproduced with great accuracy at great speed.

"During my high school days, and when I was competing at senior level, I did at least two or three hundred *uchikomi* a day," he declares. "Sometimes I did more—up to a thousand a day."

He did *uchikomi* in the various ways outlined in this chapter. As a general point, Minami recommends *uchikomi* on the move, which instills the sense of controlling a moving opponent while at the same time getting the entry right. If many training partners are available, as in Japan, then plenty of *nage-komi* (throwing practice) is invaluable. It is good to break down *morote-seoi-nage* into its component parts, both in the early days of a study and later, in order to correct faults that creep in under the pressure of *randori* and competition.

All the *uchikomi* shoud be done in a lively and realistic manner. The great temptation is to allow sluggishness to enter the practice, especially towards the end of the sets of ten or twenty. This is just a waste of time.

Weight training note: the most important weight training for *morote-seoi-nage* is, not surprisingly, the full squat. Kiyoto Katsuki a world champion and *morote-seoi-nage* specialist, was famed for being able to do a full squat with 220 kilograms. This was quite amazing considering that he was only a lightweight at 71 kg!

Hitori Uchikomi (shadow uchikomi)

For shadow uchikomi I start by developing an impression of the whole movement by myself. I ensure that the action is dynamic. And, I make sure that I cover the same amount of ground as I would with a partner.

c) Notice that as I turn, I am already pulling upwards and outwards with my *hikite*.

a) I assume an imaginary grip.

d) I make a low entry. A common mistake is to make the entry too high, which would allow *uke* to block it easily.

b) I lunge into the technique with my left leg leading.

e) I spring up to complete the exercise.

Ushiro-mawari

a) I start the step back, imagining I am bringing *uke* with me.

b) I pay particular attention to my *hikite*, executed at the same time as my right foot makes its big step.

c) I squat down into a good position—not too low but certainly not too high.

Hikite (sleeve grip)

Sometimes called the long pull. The hikite pull is particularly important in the entry of the *mae-mawari* style of *morote-seoi-nage*.

a) I begin by adopting a regular sleeve-lapel grip.

b) I pull outwards and upwards. Power comes from the base of my right foot.

c) My arm lifts high, the outside edge of the hand turning upwards. *Uke* comes onto his toes.

Tsurite (lapel grip)

Sometimes called the short pull.

a) For this exercise I only grip onto the *tsurite*. I push back fractionally in order to get a forward response from *uke*.

b) The pull coincides with the step—they take place simultaneously. I begin to wrap my wrist around his lapel.

c) I make a complete turn. Notice that my wrist and forearm is completely wrapped around *uke*'s lapel. This prevents elbow damage should *uke* pull back strongly.

San-Nin Uchikomi (three person uchikomi)

This exercise is used to develop power in the technique.

a) I step back a bit to create the momentum for turning in.

b) I begin the turn by leading with my left leg. Notice that my left foot is already turning towards the front.

c) The entry is made. I drop in low, tucked my left elbow in tightly into *uke*'s armpit and pull downwards with my *hikite* grip.

d) I load *uke* onto my back. It is useful to stay in this position for a few extra seconds, to develop strength and power.

Turning Speed

A good turn of speed in the spin is essential. This is one way of developing it while ensuring a good position with the hips.

a) I take a slight step backwards to develop the momentum for the entry. Notice that I am only hold on with the *hikite* grip. My left hand is tucked into my belt.

b) I begin the entry by leading with my left leg. My *hikite* is pulling upwards.

c) I come in squarely underneath uke. Now I begin to pull downwards with my *hikite*.

d) I turn towards my right and pull *uke's* left arm tightly over my shoulders. This is a very good entry.

Turning Speed Kogo Uchikomi (alternate uchikomi)

An effective method of developing a rounded and smooth movement in response to my partner's movement.

a) *Uke* first attacks with *osoto-gari* and I provide resistance.

b) As he comes out I continue my push.

c) Now, the space I need has been created.

d) I drop under for *morote-seoi-nage*.

A determined *morote-seoi-nage* by Minami

IPPON–SEOI-NAGE

Hidetoshi Nakanishi

Ippon-Seoi-Nage: A Personal View

Like most children in Japan, my introduction at the age of 10 to the wealth of throwing techniques in judo was *morote-seoi-nage*. I came from a sumo family—my grandfather and my uncle having both been amateur champions in my hometown of Fukuoka on the southern island of Kyushu—so combat sports were in my blood. From the start I enjyed the intense physicality of judo, the element of close contact. And there seemed nothing more satisfying than turning in under a partner, taking him on my back, and throwing him flat on the *tatami* in front of me. Yet even at that age I was acutely aware that *morote-seoi-nage*, and its sister throw, *ippon-seoi-nage*, called for high levels of skill to perform well. This offered a particular satisfaction that went beyond the simple delights of winning a small competition or throwing one of my friends in class. Even as a young boy I became fascinated by the challenge of developing that skill, and by the time I went to high school not a day would go past without at least a couple of hundred *uchikomi* at some point.

Then, as now, I was relatively short in stature (I am 168 cm) and *seoi-nage* became the obvious throw to concentrate on. I seemed to have a natural feeling for the action of "back-carry" which is the central feature of the throw—and its literal translation. I clearly didn't have the potential shape for other classes of throw such as *uchimata* or *osoto-gari*, though I learned and practised them as time went on. But I loved *seoi-nage*, to the point of

obsession. Even now, after 25 years in judo, when I am much more aware of the extraordinary range of judo *waza*, and have also developed some skill with other throws such as *sode-tsuri-komi-goshi* and *kouchi-gari*, my primary affection is for *ippon-seoi-nage*.

I used it at crucial points in my competitive career including the final of the world championships in Moscow, 1983, when I won the -71 kg category. But I must admit that my proficiency didn't come easily.

I attack Nagy of Romania with *ippon-seoi-nage*. Although he tried to hook my right leg with his right leg, in an effort to thwart the throw, I managed to rotate and throw him for *waza-ari*. 1983 Moscow World Championships.

For a start, I am pretty sure, as I look back on those early days, that despite those thousands of *uchikomi*, I didn't practise very well, and this shaped and directed my future career. *Morote-seoi-nage* relies on precision of attack, and speed of entry, but also on a certain softness and flexibility in the arms and shoulders. My personal inclination was to plunge into repetition, pushing myself and my body to the limits, and in my teens I did this with more vigour than wisdom. By paying more attention in my *morote-seoi-nage uchikomi* to power than to a more supple entry, I developed big and powerful arms and shoulders (later, my teacher at Tokai University, Nobuyuki Sato, nicknamed me *tetsujin* or "iron man") but I didn't manage to throw many people. However, I wasn't put off by this—I just decided to practise all the more. The inevitable end result was injury to my right elbow—my *tsurite* grip—which is a common complaint of many people, in Japan and elsewhere. I simply couldn't do *morote-seoi-nage*.

Ippon-seoi-nage, however, was a very different matter. Though success here didn't come quickly either. I was able to adapt my strengths and compensate for my weaknesses. I learned to put my physical strength to good use, developing an attacking style that dominated and confused my opponents. I would attack with a range of small techniques, setting them up for the particular timing I needed to enter with *ippon-seoi-nage*; and then I would explode underneath my opponents to send them over onto their backs.

I received particular inspiration when I was 14. I watched Toyokazu Nomura win the -70 kg gold medal at the Munich Olympics. He was the star of the occasion, winning all his contests with *seoi-nage* for *ippon*. In the final, he threw Antoni Zajkowski for *ippon* with a left *ippon-seoi-nage*. His technique was to be crucial for me, and I carried the image of the throw on the back of my retina for a long time.

My first real success came when I was 18 in the Kyushu Junior Championships in 1976. In the final, I faced a taller opponent who took a left high collar grip against my traditional right hand grip. Whenever I attempted to step in for left *ippon-seoi-nage*, I could feel him pulling back to destroy my technique. So I switched to *ippon-osoto-gari*, and scored *waza-ari*. In my very next attack I once again tried *ippon-osoto-gari* but I did so in the expectation that he would push and lean forward to stop it, which he kindly did—and I was already switching to normal *ippon-seoi-nage*.

Much of my judo was based upon this kind of disguise. Another important match for me was in my fourth year at Tokai University. At the All-Japan University Championships, I was captain of the team which was aiming for its fourth consecutive win. This event, one of the most important in the annual Japanese judo calendar, is an open-weight competition so at around 71kg, I was giving away quite a lot of weight. What's more, not only had I the responsibility of being captain, but we were also wthout the

In 1980 I captained the Tokai team to its fourth consecutive victory at the All-Japan University Championships.

a) Dropping onto one knee…

b) ...*ippon* scored.

benefit of our strongest competitor, Yasuhiro Yamashita.

Nevertheless, we got to the final to meet Tsukuba University. Things didn't start well. I was the first of the seven man team to fight. I faced a -95kg opponent who opened the scoring by throwing me for *yuko* with *ouchi-gari*. As the time went by and I couldn't even the score, the pressure began to mount. A loss at this stage would almost inevitably result in the loss of the title—not something that the captain of Tokai wanted to have on his record.

Almost always, at these moments of desparate need, one turns to the techniques in whichone has most faith. In my case, it was *ippon-seoi-nage*. With the match well into the last minute I started a flurry of attacks that concluded with a 100% attempt to throw my opponent. I turned left, dropped on one knee to get right under him with *ippon-seoi-nage*, then,

with him safely on my back, rose upright, gaining sufficient height to make sure that I could turn him in mid-air for *ippon*.

I called on an almost exact replica of this throw in Moscow in the final of the -71 kg category of the World Championships. I had thrown my first opponent, Nagy of Romania, with a standing *ippon-seoi-nage*. I was pleased with it because, unlike so many *ippon-seoi-nage* attacks seen at this level, I had managed to get past his defences and hoist him in the air without dropping to my knees. In fact, in my eagerness, I went a little too far through and lost a bit of control, resulting in *waza-ari* rather *ippon*. But Ezio Gamba, the reigning Olympic champion from Italy, was a very different matter. We met in the final and I knew that, as a stylist, he was not going to be easy to beat. My first attack was *ippon-seoi-nage* but there was too much space between us, and he stepped aside. A little later I attacked again. I pushed him back and stepped in—*mae-mawari* style. I dropped low on one knee and loading him onto my back. I started the lift but Gamba was not Olympic champion for nothing, and with admirable dexterity, managed to twist out of the throw, conceding only a *yuko* score. I gained *ippon* shortly after that with *kuzure-kami-shiho-gatame* after he attacked me with *morote-seoi-nage*. But the turning point of the match was my opening score.

These were the highlights of my *ippon-seoi-nage* career. But it was there as a constant theme, when I won the All-Japan weight category championships in 1982 and 1983, and the Tournoi de Paris in 1982, and in numerous other events in Japan and elsewhere.

Ippon-Seoi-Nage: The Basics

Shisei (posture)

a) This is the ideal posture for *ippon-seoi-nage*. Of course judo is all about skilful adaptation under stress, but here is what we are aiming for. It is virtually identical to the basic posture for *morote-seoi-nage*. There are three points to note about the front view:

i) My position with my feet, shoulder length apart, in a line with the shoulders of *uke*.

ii) The relative difference in height during an attack—the traditional concept is that my belt must be lower than my partner's.

iii) I am looking clearly, straight ahead. Naturally, this will change dramatically during the course of the throwing action, but the awareness of head position, and exactly where the eyes are looking, have an important part to play in an understanding of *ippon-seoi-nage*.

b) The basic posture is often likened to the skiing posture: knees bent, weight slightly forward on the toes, back straight—but with a generally light, springy feel to it, ready to catapult forward at any moment.

) By way of contrast, the bad posture.
Note the bent back, where contact with *uke*
s lost entirely, resulting in a loss of control.
With my head bent in this manner, I am not
o manoeuverable or springy.

Right Hand Grip

Because of the fact that *ippon-seoi-nage* is not a technique that employs both the *hikite* and *tsurite* grips, it is simpler to refer to the different grips as right hand grip and left hand grip.

The distinctive right hand grip for *ippon-seoi-nage* may appear to be the same in many wrestling traditions, but its judo form has a particular pattern. It is easier to see its operation with bare arms.

a) The initial lift breaks the balance and opens the space for my right arm.

b) I bring my partner's arm down sharply at the same time bringing my right arm—equally sharply—into his armpit. It should feel like a ratchet clicking into place rather than a soft blending.

 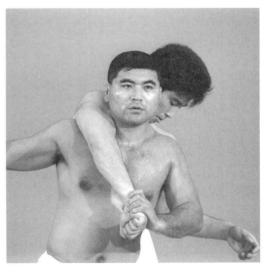

Finally, as I push his wrist even further down, I twist my right hand to bring my little finger into contact with his bicep. This has the effect of tightening up the whole grip. Speaking more anatomically, the twist of my hand brings my own bicep into its most efficient mode.

d) One of the dangers of *ippon-seoi-nage*. The arm slips over my shoulder, ruining my balance and putting me in danger of a strangle.

Left Hand Grip

The left hand grip for *ippon-seoi-nage* can be on the sleeve, the armpit or the lapel part of the *judogi*.

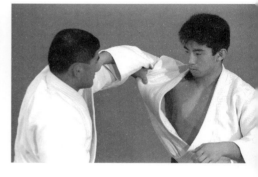

Sode (sleeve)

The basic *hikite* (pulling) grip: holding the bottom of the sleeve, little fingers grasping firmly. Though basic, it is the least effective in actual practice because it does not offer very good control of the shoulder. It is therefore more difficult to get into a good throwing position.

Waki (armpit)

Gripping the folds of the cloth by the armpit offers better control of the shoulder. It also helps to control *uke*'s arm—making it less easy for him to put his hand down to prevent a throw. The armpit grip acts like a normal sleeve-pulling (*hikite*) grip. But it is necessary to lift with the elbow to create space for the right arm—an action which also helps with the *kuzushi*. The danger of this position is that it gives *uke* the chance of *shimewaza* if the *ippon-seoi-nage* attack fails.

ri (lapel)

The lapel is generally easy to get hold of, nd offers better control of the shoulder ian the sleeve. When you have the ndergrasp *uke* has the dominant position bove your arm, and you have to lift it to et your right arm in position. *Uke* thus has ie gravity advantage. One way to combat iis is to push up with the elbow, and sing the right hand, push *uke*'s arm off bur own. Then attack immediately. This as the favoured method of the Japanese eavyweight Sumio Endo. If you saw the ze and character of his right hand, you ould understand why he had so much iccess.

b) A slightly more subtle method than Endo's is the raised wrist method, which can also give you enough space to work. This also lessens the chance of being caught with a strangle should the attack fails.

c) The most popular and successful lapel grip is when you can get the overgrasp. You will have good control over *uke*'s shoulder, and can prevent him from putting his hand out to stop the throw. There is also less chance of a strangle should the throw fail.

Dealing with Defences Againt the Right Arm

One of the most common ways of stopping a right-handed *ippon-seoi-nage* is to control th
tori's right arm, thus preventing the turn taking place at all.
Situation I:
Uke has control of my right sleeve.

a) *Uke* has taken hold of my sleeve in an effort to control my right arm.

b) I force my arm down and around hi wrist*. I try to keep *uke*'s arm extended— is weaker while it is straight.

c) Next, I begin to wind his arm inwards.

d) Now he is completely trapped—there i no escaping the *ippon*.

*At this point my hand is on the outside of his hand. Actually, I can also wind his arm i
if my hand is on the inside of his hand. It works equally effectively either way.

nusz Pawlowski of Poand throws 1987 Word Champion, Yosuke Yamamoto of Japan, by winding
e Japanese player's right arm. *Ippon* was scored, making this throw one of the biggest upsets of
e tournament. 1988 Seoul Olympics.

Situation II—I keep *uke*'s right arm away.

Situation III—Against high grip.

a) I hold his wrist and force his hands away. This gives me the space I need to turn into the techniques. The more I push the more he will push back.

a) *Uke* reaches for a high collar. Very fas this comes hard and fast, almost like blow. I block it much the same way as would in a *nage-no-kata* * situation.

b) The entry calls for timing—I let go of his wrist and turn in, under him, as he pushes into me.

b) I grab hold of his right arm an immediately turn into *ippon-seoi-nage, mae mawari* style.

*In *nage-no-kata*, *ippon-seoi-nage* i demonstrated as a response to a blow.

Ippon-Seoi-Nage: Kenka-Yotsu

Although tradition teaches us to do *ippon-seoi-nage* off the sleeve, the *kenka-yotsu* version, where the technique is done off the lapel, is actually more effective. The basic reason is that the throw is generally executed in the opposite direction to the opponent's main throwing techniques, and therefore has a good element of surprise.

The Overgrasp

I prefer the top grip for *ippon-seoi-nage*. I feel it is stronger than the undergrasp although some *ippon-seoi-nage* specialists like Toshihiko Koga, prefers the undergrasp.

b) I bring my left arm into position. I don't just slide it there: I make a forceful upwards movement, as if I were hitting the underneath of *uke*'s biceps.

If I take a right grip, and my opponent is left, I allow him to take the inside grip. He thinks that he has effectively stopped my right-handed attacks. But with this grip I can go left—and fast. This is the basic principle behind the *kenka-yotsu ippon-seoi-nage*.

a) I get the overgrasp. Notice the bent wrist lifting action. This gives a more powerful lift than with a stiff straight wrist. It helps with the *kuzushi* if you accentuate this lifting action in *uchikomi*.

c) Finally, I click my arm into place.

The undergrasp

The undergrasp has the advantage of allowing you to lift up his arm easily. However there is also the danger of a *shimewaza* if your attack fails.

a) I adopt an undergrasp.

b) This grip allows me to raise his arms very high. As with the overgrasp, I bend my wrist.

c) I turn into position and pull his arm down.

d) I click my arm into place.

Ippon-Seoi-Nage: Special Variations

Ushiro-Mawari (Reverse Turn)

n Japan this is generally the first *ippon-seoi-nage* to be taught, as it gives a good opportunity to grasp the basics.

Ai-yotsu
) Taking the standard grip, I retreat in step with *uke*.

) I take a large step with my left foot and tart to draw *uke* forwards with a strong ull on his sleeve.

c) My strong pull has brought him well onto his right foot. I turn in front of him, putting my right foot in line with my left. Note that there is still a small gap between us so that I can complete the *kuzushi* with a little extra pull once my right hand encircles his bicep and takes effect.

d) I bring him directly forward.

e) I unload him with an added twisting action. I aim to put him down in the area in front of my left foot.

Kenka-yotsu

This is a very effective version of the throw. In this version I throw to the left, off my *tsurite* grip.

a) I get *uke* to come forward. As I retreat I control his left shoulder with my right hand. I want to feel him pressing against my hand, so that when I begin the technique, he will be pulled off-balanced quite easily.

b) I begin the turn by pulling back with my right leg and lifting upwards with my *tsurite*.

c) I drop under him. Notice that *uke* falls right onto my back.

d) I load him completely onto my back…

e) …and unload him by straightening my legs.

Mae-Mawari (front turn)

This is a faster entry but slightly more difficult than *ushiro-mawari*.

a) I step in with my right foot, while at exactly the same time lifting high with my sleeve grip.

b) I bring my left foot behind me into throwing position as I turn in under the arm.

c) I hoist *uke* onto my back…

d) …and unload him off my back.

Moving to my right

The stepping pattern for this timing is slightly different. It is a fast and direct entry.

a) I draw *uke* with my tsurite and begin moving towards my right.

b) I move in such a way that he is just a little bit ahead of me.

c) I pivot on my right leg and turn in for the attack. Notice that I'm dropping down low to get him onto my back.

d) I straighten up and throw him over.

Moving to my left

Although this technique is demonstrated moving to my left, the entry can actually be adapted for many other angles.

a) I begin moving towards my left.

b) This time I am the one who moves just a little bit ahead.

c) I pivot on my left leg and turn in for the technique.

d) I get down low and bend forward. The combination of my sudden forward drop and the leftward movement breaks *uke's* balance and loads him onto my back easily

Tsugi-Ashi: Leg-in-Between

An uncompromising competition technique emphasizing power and effectiveness.

) The gripping is hard. I take a stance, ight foot forward.

c) I begin the power lift. My feet are not parallel to *uke*'s as in the traditional *ippon-seoi-nage*. This is an important competition variation.

) Suddenly, I make a deep entry in etween uke's legs. I twist at the hips to ook the other way, simultaneously ringing my right arm into *ippon-seoi-nage* osition.

d) I drive off the back leg, for extra power...

e) ...and, launch *uke* over the top.

Bounce-Reaction

There is a certain amount of power here, but really it is a timing technique.

Version I

a) I begin by pulling *uke* forwards and downwards. The back of his collar is like a rope around his neck. This very uncomfortable position makes him want to straighten up.

b) The moment he does so, I turn in for the entry.

c) I drop down low.

d) He is completely loaded onto my back and can be easily thrown over.

·rsion II

We are in an extreme *kenka-yotsu* :uation. I push down hard against *uke*'s)ow. This forces *uke* to bend downwards.

b) Suddenly I release the pressure and lift upwards with my *tsurite* grip.

I enter immediately into the technique…

d) …and throw him over.

The Clamp

This is particularly common in the powerful style of Western judo, though it is seen Japan as well.

a) I put my right arm into *ippon-seoi-nage* making no attempt to turn.

b) I clamp on to *uke*'s arm, pulling him in to me. I have control of him and can take him in any direction I feel like.

c) I shoulder charge, pushing him back to create space for my hips.

Now I can turn. Here I drop down very
.w.

I immediately spring up again.

drove forward and throw *uke* towards
y right.

Drop Knee Ippon-Seoi-Nage

This is a very hard throw—clearly aiming for an *ippon*.

a) I make a low drop onto one knee.

b) I bend forward to load him onto r back.

c) I spring forward and upwards off my right knee to gain the height necessary. This is very explosive, like a sprinter coming off his blocks.

d) I do a forward roll in mid air. Tl absolutely smashes *uke* to the *tatami*.

Ippon-Seoi-Otoshi: Standing Version-Leg Block

I make a fast entry—*mae-mawari* style.

In order to drop low underneath *uke*, I etch out my right leg, blocking his legs.

He is not loaded or hoisted onto my ck—I simply trip him over my extended ht leg. That is why it is called *seoi-otoshi*.

Ippon-Seoi-Otoshi: Drop Version-Two Knees

a) I make a quick spin as I drop. My turn is completed while my knees are still in the air. The sheer weight of my body breaks *uke*'s balance. Notice that he is already tipping forward.

b) I begin to pull him over.

c) He is pulled completely onto his back. There is no attempt to spring upwards, hence the name *seoi-otoshi*.

Janusz Pawlowski of Poland attacks Br Cooper of New Zealand with a right-sid *ippon-seoi-otoshi* on both knees.

Ippon-Seoi-Otoshi: Drop Version-Single Knee

[make a fast *mae-mawari* entry leading
h my right leg.

b) As I turn I drop onto my right knee.

Ike is tipped forward and onto my back.

d) However, instead of springing upwards,
I just pull downwards.

Soto-Muso

A small but useful little addition to an *ippon-seoi-nage* armoury. It has its origins in *su* where this kind of flick is still used today.

Standing Version

a) I make my entry.

b) *Uke* threatens to come around my hip respond by extending my right arm wid

c) My arm can merely act as a block, or it can actually help with the sweep.

d) *Uke* stumbles over my right arm. T throw has been referred to as a kind of *se otoshi*.

Drop Version

I drop down into the *seoi-otoshi* position.

b) Next, I extend my right arm and block his leg.

As I spring upwards, *uke* is wheeled over ry right hand.

d) He is thrown flat on his back.

attack Danielli of France with a drop-
own version of *soto-muso*. 1982 Tournoi de
aris.

Ippon-Seoi-Nage Counter to Ouchi-Gari

a) My opponent attacks with *ouchi-gari*.

b) I step off it, lifting my leg. I begin to lift my right arm.

c) I begin the turn pivoting on my left leg. This is an *ushiro-mawari* entry.

d) I drop down low, bringing him onto my back…

e) …and throw him for *ippon*!

Ippon-Seoi Nage against Defence to Ippon-Seoi-Nage

his calls for good balance and a heightened awareness in mid-technique—but is required
all top fighters.

I come in for *ippon-seoi-nage. Uke* defends
bringing his left leg over my left thigh
d hooks in.

b) I let go of the *hikite* grip so that I can grab
hold of his leg.

I continue with the attack, using my left
n to disentangle his leg from my leg.

d) I throw him off to my right side.

Combinations into Ippon-Seoi-Nage

Sutemi-kouchi into ippon-seoi-nage

Sometimes *uke* manages to resist the *sutemi-kouchi* but cannot break free. This is the answer although it calls for considerable power.

a) I have come in with *sutemi-kouchi* but *uke* has resisted successfully.

b) I start to stand up and turn around. In doing so, I hold on to *uke*'s right leg and actually begn to lift it.

c) I bring my left leg back to be in line with my right. This gives me the turn and lift I need. My right hand is still holding on to his right leg. Now, he is loaded on my back.

Kosoto-Gari into Ippon-Seoi-Nage

This technique is done from a *kenka-yotsu* situation. A committed initial attack is necessary.

) I attack *uke* with a *kosoto-gari*. My body weight bears on his left shoulder and arm.

) He extracts his left leg.

Now I have the space I need to make my ntry.

d) I begin turning into the throw, pivoting on my left leg.

e) I load him onto my back.

f) And, over he goes!

Osoto-Gari into Seoi-Nage

This is usually done from a *kenka-yotsu* grip.

I attack with an *osoto-gari* from an *ippon-oi-nage* grip. It must be a realistic attack in der to get him to react by pushing rwards, against me.

b) As soon as I feel his committed resistance, I change directions but my left leg is still hooked around his left leg.

Next, I extend my left leg and begin to ll him over.

d) He is tripped over my extended left leg: *seoi-otoshi*!

Combinations from Ippon-Seoi-Nage

Ippon-Seoi-Nage into Sutemi-Kouchi

When I was 16 and still in high school, my *sensei*, Yasuichi Matsumoto, an All-Japan champion, told me to master this technique. He saw that despite the hundreds of *uchikomi* I did on *ippon-seoi-nage*, I wasn't having much success with it in competition. When I won it was usually because of my fighting spirit more than technique. He told me that this throw was a complement to *ippon-seoi-nage*. He the got his great friend, Hideo Yamamoto, a acknowledged master of this technique send me a book he had written. Yamamoto *sensei* sent me the book together with personal note of encouragement. I studie this technique and two months later, in major tournament, I threw an opponent fc *ippon* with it!

Ai-yotsu.
This is a direct attack done with an *ushir mawari* turn.
a) I face *uke* squarely, in a slight *ai-yots* stance.

b) I pull him onto me as if I were doir *kouchi-gari*.

c) As I hook in, I grab his right thigh.

d) Next, I charge forward, in a sacrificing motion—hence the name *sutemi-kouchi*.

e) I land on top of *uke* to ensure the *ippon*.

Kenka-yotsu
This is a double-motion attack done with a *mae-mawari* turn.
a) I turn in for an *ippon-seoi-nage* attack but *uke* is resisting strongly.

b) I come out...

c) I am now ready for my second attack.

d) I lunge right in with the *sutemi-kouchi*…

e) …trapping *uke*'s right leg and taking him straight down.

f) Ippon is inevitable.

Ippon-Seoi-Nage into Ouchi-Gari

Though this technique lacks a *tsurite* grip, it works quite well because of the element of surprise.

a) I make a feint *ippon-seoi-nage* attack.

b) However, instead of turning completely I hook in with my right leg for an *ouchi-gari* instead. It is important to continue pulling in tightly with my right arm.

c) I drive forwards with my left leg…

d) …and take *uke* down.

Ippon-Seoi-Nage into Osoto-Gari

) I come in for what seems to be like an *ppon-seoi-nage* attack.

) However instead of rotating fully, I witch it to *osoto-gari*. I hook in tightly vith my left leg and grab hold of his high with my left hand.

) I finish the throw by reaping with both iy left hand and left leg.

Three Attacks from an Ippon-Seoi-Nage Grip

When coming in for an *ippon-seoi-nage* it is possibleto do three different but related attacks.

Kosoto-Gari
American world champion, Michael Swain, demonstrates this sequence.

a) Swain comes in for what seems like an *ippon-seoi-nage* attack.

b) He continues with the *ippon-seoi-nage* grip but notice that he is ready to reap with is left leg.

c) *Uke's* reaction and Swain's big reap makes the technique work.

ani-Otoshi

) I come in for an *ippon-seoi-nage* attack
vith my arms but my legs are ready for
ifferent attack.

) I reach out and attack both his legs.
Notice that both of *uke*'s legs are off the
round.

) I sacrifice by going to the ground with
im.

Ura-Nage

a) Yuri Sokolov, a former world champion from the Soviet Union, attacks his opponent with what looks like an *ippon-seoi-nage*. However, notice that his left leg is behind *uke*'s right leg.

b) As his opponent lifts his right leg up to avoid the attack, Sokolov begins the lift.

c) Sokolov arches backwards and completely picks his opponent up!

Overshoot

uite often in doing *ippon-seoi-nage*, you overshoot your hips. Below are three ways to ake the most of this situation.

pon-seoi-nage into kata-guruma

his may appear like an entangled technique but it works.

a) I turn in for an *ippon-seoi-nage*.

b) I have overshot and my hips are way out. I make the most of the situation by reaching for his right leg with my right hand.

c) I pick him up. An unusual *kata-guruma*.

Ippon-seoi-nage into kuchiki-daoshi

a) I spin in for a *ippon-seoi-nage*.

b) I have overshot again. As with the *kata-guruma* attack, I reaching for his right leg

c) I grab hold of it but instead of picking him up, I charge forwards, still holding onto his left collar with my right hand.

d) I pull up his right leg as he fall backwards. This ensures a hard fall.

pon-seoi-nage into morote-gari

I rotate strongly for *ippon-seoi-nage*.

b) This time I have done a full overshoot.

I grab hold of both of his legs...

d) ...and charge forwards.

Defences

a) The safest defence against *ippon-seoi-nage* is not to let it get going in the first place. Grip therefore, are the initial line of defence. By pinning the *tsurite* arm into the side of you opponent, you can stop the turn dead.

a) But, if your opponent has managed to turn, keep pushing the elbow away from you, and most importantly, turn sideways, taking the right leg back. Don't let your arm get trapped—it is crucial to keep on pushing. This has the effect of preventing contact between your chest and your opponent's back—and avoiding the danger of being caught by a *kouchi-gari* counter.

b) The second stage is to tear your *hikite* hand free.

c) Lower your weight by bending your knees—and push your knees into your opponent's buttocks. Not a very pleasant thing to do, but it works, and may dissuade your opponent from trying the technique again.

Counters

Sukui-Nage I

There are a number of counter throw opportunities. They are easier to do against standing *ippon-seoi-nage*. But they also work against drop *seoi-nage* when the attacker tries to drive off his knees to make the throw as demonstrated here. It is possible to anticipate that drive, and use sukui-nage. This is also called *te-guruma*.

a) I keep low—note that I do not bend over, but try to keep a straight back—and grasp the cloth at the inner thigh.

b) I stand up and wheel *uke* over, my left hand going higher than my right in a circular action. The direction of the wheel will vary.

c) Note the action of the right hand, pulling up sharply to spin *uke* onto his back; the feeling is almost like throwing a knife!

Sukui-Nage II

This demonstration was done with a little bit too much vigour, but the principle of the pendulum swing can be clearly seen.

This not only offers a counter—but also prevents you being caught with *sutemi kouchi* if your opponent makes sudden switch.

a) My opponent attacks. I want to counter, so I reach to pick up the inside of his trouser leg. The lifting of my right leg is a safeguard against *sutemi-kouchi*.

b) The lift…

c) …the turn.

d) *Uke* is thrown cleanly to the ground.

Note: The pendulum effect of my leg swinging back to the ground helps generate the necessary lift to pick up and throw *uke*.

Ippon-Seoi-Nage: Training

Most of the formal training for *ippon-seoi-nage* follows the patterns outlined in the *morote-seoi-nage* training chapter. Uchikomi the backbone, as it is with all judo techniques. All the variations of uchikomi need to be practised regularly. Static uchikomi forms the basis, and allows particular attention to be paid to specific points such as the breaking of *uke's* balance, the turn, and the ideal positioning both slowly and also at speed.

Knowing What to Focus On

Prior to each set, you should decide on which aspect of the throw to focus on—*kite* or *tsurite*, the spin turn, or the body position, or even speed. It is also possible to decide to focus on the overall feeling of the *ippon-seoi-nage* movement, rather than a single element. But the important thing is to decide what to focus on, rather than vaguely making one entry or another in the blind hope that it will do something for your *ippon-seoi-nage*.

The particular point that is often overlooked is the use of the eyes. When you attack, you should be aware where you are going to deposit your opponent—directly behind you or to one side, or off at an angle. Of course this is more than likely to change as *uke* moves and alters his position and his defence; but if, as you turn, you are preparing to look at the spot where you want to throw, your turn will probably be faster, and the throwing action more accurate.

Uchikomi

Mae-mawari and *ushiro-mawari* turns must become second nature. Certain *uchikomi* routines can concentrate on alternating entries of each type, and even adding directions to one side or another. All this trains the balance and will promote good reflexes—even automatic reflexes, so that you can attack with *ippon-seoi-nage* at any and every moment.

It is necessary to start most training sessions with smooth, steady rhythmic *uchikomi* movements, looking at details. At first, work with a three-step pattern, but gradually cut down the steps so that you can whirl in the second *uke* shifts his balance. A *dan* grade working at reasonable speed should be able to achieve 60 *uchikomi* a minute—with full accuracy.

Shadow *uchikomi*, three-person *uchikomi*, alternate *uchikomi*, *nage-komi* (throwing practice)—they should all be part of a daily routine. Before competitions I did huge numbers of *nage-komi*. In Japan we have the great advantage of having many training partners, so *nage-komi* for 30 minutes is not a problem...except that it is exhausting.

Mental Training

This is more difficult to write about. To develop a throw to a high standard it is important to develop and understanding of the details, as well as the instinctive feeling for it. The imaginative faculty is very strong, and can feed into the general body movement. You must be able to imagine yourself throwing, and know what it feels like at every stage. Imagine yourself slip past a defensive arm in *kenka-yotsu* stance, stepping across into the technique. Imagine the feeling of moving in right-hand stance but switching left as your opponent moves in response.

A more conceptual approach can be used as well. If you meet an opponent with a wide stance—what do you do? Or an opponent with a very one-sided stance? Someone who professes to have *ippon-seoi-nage* as his or her *tokui-waza* (favourite technique) should be able to have an immediate answer for all eventualities. This is not to say that they will always work—but the theory should be correct. In short, both the conceptual and the instinctive faculties must be used—and both can be trained.

Fighting Spirit

At Tokai University we feel it is very important to practice *randori* with bigger men, even if we compete in weight categories. As Minami said, this is very important for *seoi-nage* specialists for technical reasons. But it is also important to develop a strong heart in competition. Every day, when I was a competitor I made sure I trained with Yasuhiro Yamashita even though he was about 125 kilos and I was 71 kilos. This taught me to keep moving. The only way a small man can overcome a big man is to catch him on the move; and quite soon it becomes second nature to move well and attack frequently but sensibly. Another training method I used was to handicap myself, especially against weaker or less experienced opponents. I would limit myself to particular throws or let him get his favoured grip, and then see how I could work around it. *Randori* is, after all, training.

Solitary practice outside the dojo

1. Inner tube

The inner tube is a useful device, especial in areas where there is a shortage training partners, or where the dojo is fi away. A daily practice of 5 x 20 repetitior in one direction is a worthwhile set. Ad other directions as fitness and smoothne improves.

2. Weights

Weight training was an essential ar regular part of my training whe I w competing. I used dumbells to improve m arm-strength for *kuzushi*. I worked with kg or 25 kg dumbbells, swinging them reps of 20, for four or five sets.

High cleans are essential to develc general body strength, and especially goc for the lower back. I had a maximum of kg, so I worked with 60 kg weights— reps, five sets. Every other day, I wou alternate with squats. Squats a particularly relevant to *seoi-nage* developing strong legs. My maximum w 150 kg, so I worked with 110 kg, 4 x repetitions.

3. Daily physical training

Most mornings at Tokai University beg with a run. We run for around 20 minut out into the country side or a park f cardio-vascular training. Invariably, v run to a temple area where there are ste; up to the building, and we will stop he for special exercises. We each carry partner up the steps, either on the back holding them in front. Sometimes we rac sometimes we go for endurance. An

Seoi up the temple steps.
A variation that is helpful for building strength
d endurance.

c) Once I reach the top, by the temple bell, I
don't rest—I immediately go into squats with my
partner on my shoulders.

metimes we race without being
eighted down by a partner.

ll squats with a partner on the shoulders
  particularly useful for *seoi-nage*
ecialists.

are *usagi-tobi* (bunny hops) although it
  important to remember that children
ly go half-way down to protect their
ees. I would do sets of 20 bunny hops,
rning in an *ushiro-mawari* pattern and
llow it up with 20 in a *mae-mawari*
ttern.
ess-ups, sit-ups, squat-thrusts and other
ercises are incorporated too. Then, after
minutes or so, we run back. This
ining process is forged of a *seoi-nage*
ecialist in Japan.

A determined *ippon-seoi-nage by me.*

COMPETITION SEOI-NAGE

Competition Judo

Britain's Neil Adams was without a doubt, one of the most accomplished judo technicians of the 1980's. In 1984, at the peak of his powers, he was on his way to an Olympic gold medal in Los Angeles. He was halfway through his final against an unknown Frank Wieneke of West Germany and looked as if he would coast to victory. Standing near the edge of the mat, he was attacked with a one-handed *uchimata* by Wieneke. Because the German only had one hand on Adams, the technique was easily squashed. However, Wieneke had the presence of mind to quickly switch the attack into a drop *ippon-seoi-nage*. He scored and for the first—and only—time in his illustrious career, Neil Adams was thrown for *ippon*.

The story didn't quite finish there. Four years later, Frank Wieneke found himself in the final of the Seoul Olympic Games. He faced not Adams, but Waldemar Legien of Poland—a fellow *ippon-seoi-nage* specialist. Like Wieneke, Legien also dropped to the left whenever he attempted his technique. The two exchanged attacks

Frank Wieneke learned what it is like to lose a Olympic final when Waldemar Legien threw hi with a magnificent *ippon-seoi-nage* for *ippon*.

in a lively contest but no points was score by either men. With just 14 seconds left the match, Wieneke, who was in dominating position in ground wor suddenly stood up. As both men came grips, Legien dropped down and thre him with an incredibly low left *ippon-se nage* that caused the German's legs to sp wildly in the air. He landed flat on his ba and *ippon* was scored.

a) Wieneke attacks with a left *uchimata*.

b) He immediately spins into a right *ippon-seoi-nage*.

c) Adams is loaded onto Wieneke's back.

d) Ippon!

haps the most oustanding exponent of *morote-seoi-nage* is the great Shozo Fujii who won every World Championships from 1971 to 1979—mainly with *morote-seoi-nage*!

ujii drops to one knee in attacking his Bulgarian onent, Welschev. Notice that Fujii has dropped well erneath his opponent—so much so that the garian has almost slipped in front of Fujii.

b) Fujii springs up.

oth men are airborne—such is the power ujii's upward drive.

d) The Bulgarian is smashed flat on his back. An indisputable *ippon*!

hihiko Koga, who does his *ippon-seoi-e* standing up, is regarded by many to the most remarkable *ippon-seoi-nage* onent in recent memory. However, at very few people know is that Koga's 1ous *ippon-seoi-nage* actually started out a complement to *sutemi-kouchi*—his ourite technique as a teenager. It was y later, as an adult that *ippon-seoi-nage* w to become his main technique.

Koga executing a dynamic *kouchi-makikomi* on his opponent from Hong Kong. 1989 Belgrade World Championships.

Nomura throwing with *morote-seoi-nage*.

Nomura thowing with *ippon-seoi-nage*.

Although *morote-seoi-nage* and *ippon-seoi-nage* are sister throws, there are many differences in the two techniques. This is evident by the fact that there are few players who can do both techniques competently. I could never do *morote-seoi-nage*...neither could Koga or Legien or Wieneke. Likewise, Minami did not do *ippon-seoi-nage*. Neither did Fujii or Angelo Parisi. However, one man—Toyokazu Nomura was an exception. Winner of the 1972 Olympic -70 kg category, Nomura won all his fights leading to the final by *ippon* using *seoi-nage*: sometimes *morote-seoi-nage* to the right, sometimes *ippon-seoi-nage* to the left. It was an unbeatable combination. In the final, he faced Zajkowski of Poland. He feinted with a right *morote-seoi-nage* but quickly spun left for *ippon-seoi-nage*. *Ippon* was scored in 27 seconds. Nomura went on to win the world title the following year, in Lausanne, in much the same way.

Although the *seoi-nages* that are usual done by women tend to be the drop-do form, over the years there have been a fe players, East and West, who ha developed standing versions of th popular throw.

a) Fumiko Ezaki of Japan throws Stavria Greece with a standing *morote-seoi-nage* ippon. 1989 Belgrade World Championships.

Catherine Arnaud of France throws Miriam Blas of Spain with a magnificent standing *ippon-na* for *ippon*. 1989 World Championships.

Elvis Gordon drops onto his right knee.
ce his unusual grip.

b) He loads Tybus onto his back by bending forward and downwards…

…and completes the throw by rolling
ards.

Elvis Gordon, England's world silver medallist and European champion had his own form of drop *ippon-seoi-nage* which he used with considerable success throughout his long career. He developed an unusual style. Facing a right-hander, he would take the overgrip with his left hand, seizing the lapel. Then, with his right hand, he took the opponent's right sleeve. Only when he had this unusual grip would he turn, drop and throw. The effect was surprising. At first it didn't seem dangerous. The opponent was often left standing on his feet, convinced that the main thrust of the attack had failed. But suddenly Gordon would pull down sharply on the sleeve, twist and turn, and the opponent would find himself thrown over—as in these pictures.

Index